A Family in Taiwan

The author would like to give special thanks to Karen S. Chung
for her valuable assistance.

LIBRARY OF CONGRESS CATALOGING-IN-PUBLICATION DATA

Yu, Ling.
 A family in Taiwan/Ling Yu; photographs by Chen Ming-jeng.
 p.   cm.
 Summary: Presents life in Taiwan as seen through the daily life of
a twelve-year-old and her family.
 1. Taiwan—Social life and customs—1975—Juvenile literature.
2. Family—Taiwan—Juvenile literature. [1. Family life—Taiwan.
2. Taiwan—Social life and customs.] I. Chen, Ming-jeng, ill.
II. Title.
DS799.845.Y8 1990   951.24'905—dc20   89-48591
                                                 CIP
                                                 AC

ISBN 0-8225-1685-3

Manufactured in the United States of America

1 2 3 4 5 6 7 8 9 10 99 98 97 96 95 94 93 92 91 90

A Family in Taiwan

Ling Yu

Photographs by Chen Ming-jeng

Lerner Publications Company · Minneapolis

PEOPLE'S
REPUBLIC
OF
CHINA

KINMEN ISLAND

TAIWAN STRAIT

PENGHU ISLAND

EAST ASIA

TAIWAN

Chang Fang-hsin is 12 years old and in the sixth grade. She lives on the first floor of a six-story apartment building near downtown Taipei, Taiwan, with her father, mother, younger sister, and two-year-old brother.

Chinese people put their family name or "last name" first, so everybody's name in the family starts with *Chang*, except for Fang-hsin's mother's. Women usually do not change their names when they marry, and Fang-hsin's mother's name is Lin Fen-hsia. But sometimes women use the title *Mrs.* with their husband's family name. So Lin Fen-hsia is also called *Mrs. Chang*.

MATSU ISLAND

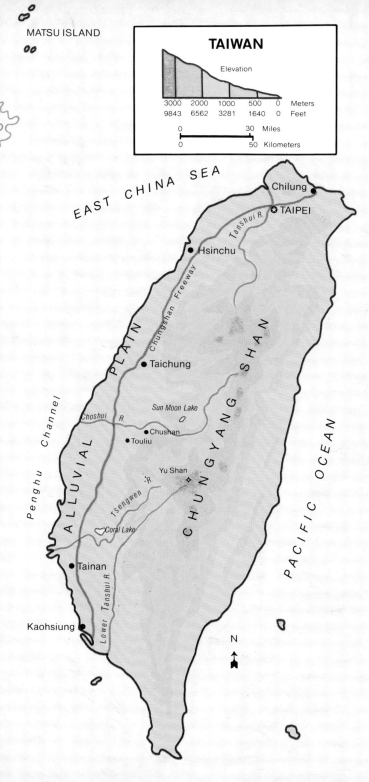

TAIWAN

Elevation

| 3000 | 2000 | 1000 | 500 | 0 | Meters |
| 9843 | 6562 | 3281 | 1640 | 0 | Feet |

0   30   Miles
0   50   Kilometers

EAST CHINA SEA

Chilung

✛ TAIPEI

Tanshui R.

Hsinchu

Chungshan Freeway

ALLUVIAL PLAIN

Taichung

Sun Moon Lake

Choshui R.

Chushan

Touliu

CHUNGYANG SHAN

Yu Shan

Tsengwen R.

Coral Lake

Tainan

Lower Tanshui R.

Kaohsiung

Penghu Channel

PACIFIC OCEAN

N

Taiwan is an island located about 120 miles (192 kilometers) off the southeastern coast of Asia. Taiwan and mainland China were once under one government called the Republic of China, which was founded in 1912. China has been a divided country since 1949.

Taiwan and some other nearby islands are under the government of the Republic of China and mainland China is under the government of the People's Republic of China.

Taiwan is very mountainous, but the capital city, Taipei, is built on a big, flat basin, which once was a huge lake. It is a busy and crowded city.

Most parts of Taiwan are hot and humid in the summer, and chilly and damp in the winter.

Fang-hsin's father goes swimming at a nearby sports club at half past five every morning. The rest of the family gets up at about six. Breakfast this morning is rice porridge with lots of side dishes—dried shredded pork, peanuts, and leftovers from the night before. Some mornings the family has rolls and milk for breakfast.

Fang-hsin speaks Mandarin (the Chinese national language) at school and with most of her friends. But she also speaks another dialect of Chinese at home called Southern Fukienese or Taiwanese. Mandarin and Taiwanese are about as different from each other as Spanish and French.

Fang-hsin is wearing a school uniform. Each grade has its own uniform, and a special uniform is worn on days that students have physical education class.

Fang-hsin walks to school with her younger sister, Pao-chen, who is in the fourth grade. It takes them about 15 minutes to walk to school. They see some friends along the way, so they all walk together.

Traffic is heavy and fast wherever you go in Taipei, so Fang-hsin is always careful when she crosses a street. So many cars in a small area make the air polluted and hot.

Fang-hsin's school is large, and she has over 40 class-mates. She helps clean the classroom and water plants as soon as she arrives. The teacher puts on an English language teaching tape so interested students can get a head start on their English.

Every morning, the whole school participates in a flag-raising ceremony. The students sing the national anthem of the Republic of China. Then they listen to a speech by the principal encouraging them to be hardworking students. Students might also go to the microphone and read compositions or recite poetry.

Fang-hsin goes to school Monday through Saturday. Most adults work a half-day on Saturdays, too. Fang-hsin has classes in Chinese, math, science, social studies, physical education, and art. Art is her favorite subject.

One day in art class she learned how to cook sugar syrup to make candy figures. This is an old Chinese folk art. The most fun was eating the figure she made after it was done!

Sometimes different classes compete with each other in sports. Today the third graders are having a tug-of-war.

At noontime, the students line up to get their lunch boxes. Fang-hsin's mother always makes an extra amount of food for Fang-hsin's and Pao-chen's lunches when she cooks supper. She packs a portion of cooked meat and vegetables over some cooked rice in a covered metal lunch box. The lunch boxes are collected in the morning and, shortly before lunch, are placed in a steamer to heat the food. Some of Fang-hsin's classmates buy a hot lunch packed in a Styrofoam box from the school.

Fang-hsin usually uses chopsticks, but a spoon can be more convenient with a lunch box. After eating, the students take a short nap at their desks.

In physical education class, the students are learning the traditional Chinese lion dance. People carry a colorful lion costume and make the lion do tricks, like playing with a ball. The lion dance symbolizes celebration, joy, and good luck and is performed at major festivals.

In this afternoon's science class, the students go outside to record the position of the sun on paper sundials they made. They use compasses to make sure they place the sundials in the same position each time.

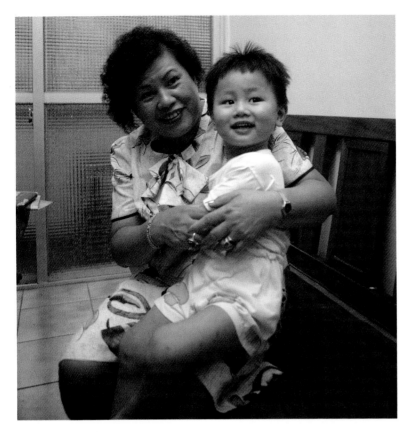

Mr. and Mrs. Chang both work during the day. So while Fang-hsin and Pao-chen are at school, a woman named Mrs. Cheng stays with Fang-hsin's little brother, Ming-hsiu.

Mrs. Chang works for the government. Her department is part of the Ministry of Finance and is in charge of regulating stock and bond investments. Many new investment companies have been set up recently, so Mrs. Chang is especially busy.

Mr. Chang has two jobs. He helps with his father's business of making concrete electric poles and he manages a food canning company.

The company has factories that process and can bamboo shoots, water chestnuts, mushrooms, unusual fruits like lychees and loquats, and other foods as well. They also freeze bamboo shoots and snow peas. The company exports its products around the world to be sold in supermarkets and to Oriental restaurants.

Mr. Chang usually works in his Taipei office, but he goes to the factories in central Taiwan at least once a week to make sure everything is running smoothly.

Mrs. Chang hurries home from work every evening to cook supper. First she cooks rice in an electric rice cooker. Then she washes and cuts lots of fresh vegetables and slices meat. She stir-fries the meat and some of the vegetables in hot oil in a wok, a bowl-shaped frying pan. She also steams whole fish with scallions, ginger, and oil, and cooks a bean curd and miso soup. Chinese people usually have soup with their meals instead of a beverage. The Changs don't often eat sweets. They have fruit for dessert instead.

The first thing Fang-hsin and Pao-chen do when they get home is take showers. Then they begin their homework.

Children in Taiwan are assigned lots of homework, starting from the first grade. They have a big monthly exam in all subjects, so everybody becomes used to tests and hard study very early. Everybody has to finish junior high school in Taiwan, but a student must pass a difficult exam to be allowed to go on to senior high school.

If Fang-hsin and Pao-chen finish their homework before supper is ready, they may watch a children's program on TV, such as a cartoon or a dramatized Chinese folk tale.

Fang-hsin can read, as well as hear, what people on TV are saying because most programs have subtitles. This is one way Fang-hsin learns how to read new Chinese characters. Another way she learns new Chinese characters is by reading the *Mandarin Daily*, a newspaper that contains news, stories, and activities especially for children.

The article shown invites students to send in their own stories. Some of the stories, and photographs of the students, will be printed in this section of the newspaper.

Mr. Chang has a business appointment, so he's not eating with the family tonight. A cousin of Fang-hsin's who goes to a technical school often eats and stays with the Changs on the weekends. After supper, everybody watches the news on TV.

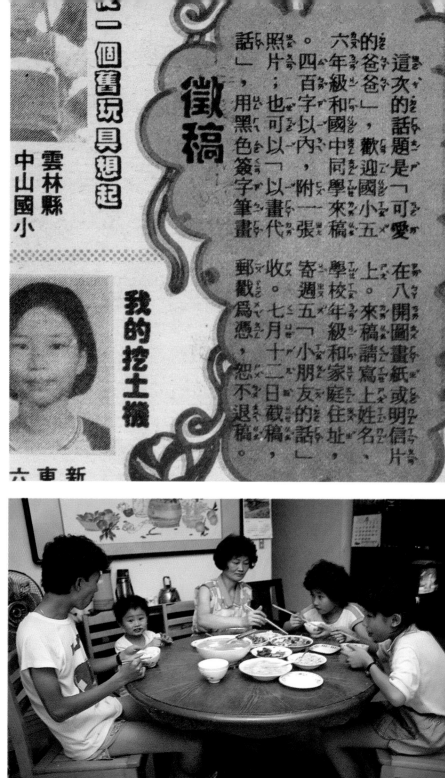

One night a week, Fang-hsin goes to a class at a neighbor's apartment to learn how to do calculations quickly with an abacus. The abacus is a very old Chinese invention.

Fang-hsin is practicing multiplication problems. Her teacher tells the students that the best and fastest abacus is the one in their heads. Once they've learned to use an abacus well, they can do all their figuring on the abacus in their heads instead of using their fingers.

During her free time, Fang-hsin likes to read stories or science books, or watch TV. Sometimes friends come over and they play with dolls. Or they might play hopscotch or Chinese jump rope, which the Chinese call "jumping rubber bands." Fang-hsin likes to play the electric organ, too.

This Saturday is the annual Dragon Boat Festival, and everyone gets the day off. Fang-hsin is excited because the whole family is going to watch the Dragon Boat races. One of Fang-hsin's friends has an older brother on the Hsin Tien township team. The races are held in several locations and commemorate the famous poet Ch'ü Yüan, who lived about 2,000 years ago. Ch'ü Yüan was a patriotic statesman and a highly revered poet.

One important part of the Dragon Boat Festival is making and eating *tsung tzu*. To make tsung tzu, these friends of Mrs. Chang place glutinous (sticky) rice on the ends of bamboo leaves. They add either a meat or a sweet filling, wrap the leaves, and then steam them.

Another Dragon Boat Festival tradition is the wearing of colorful sachets. A sachet is a packet of fragrant herbs that is worn around the neck. Long ago, wearing a sachet was thought to ward off evil spirits. Fang-hsin made a sachet at school, but she's picking out another ready-made one at the market with her mother. It smells somewhat like curry.

The most exciting part of the holiday is the dragon boat races. The colorfully painted boats are propelled by teams representing different districts of the Taipei area. A drummer in each boat pounds out a rhythm to which the paddlers stroke. One man in each boat climbs to the very front of the boat. His sole duty is to grab a flag at the finish line.

The Changs watch from near the finish line. It's a close race but the Hsin Tien team moves out ahead and finishes first!

July is graduation time. The fifth graders place flower wreaths over the heads of the graduates as each one enters the auditorium. The principal and some teachers, parents, and local government officials give speeches wishing the graduates good luck. Gifts are presented to each of the graduates. Fang-hsin receives an award and a special gift for being among the top three students in her class.

The fifth graders have made flower arches that the sixth-grade graduates pass through at the end of the ceremony.

Fang-hsin still has homework to do during summer vacation. Assignments are printed in a book that every student takes home. Fang-hsin keeps a diary of what she does every day. She also writes three pages a week of calligraphy with a brush pen.

This is Fang-hsin's name written in Chinese calligraphy with a brush pen. The tiny symbols to the upper right of each larger character are part of the *Mandarin Phonetic Symbols*. The symbols tell how to pronounce the characters. Many books for children, as well as Fang-hsin's newspaper, use these symbols alongside regular Chinese characters.

This summer Fang-hsin and Pao-chen visit their grandparents in central Taiwan. Fang-hsin loves to visit them because there she has cousins to play with and lots of room to ride her bike, and the air is very fresh.

Fang-hsin's paternal grandparents (her father's parents) live in a small town in central Taiwan called Chushan. Grandfather Chang helped design the large modern house they live in.

The town is called Chushan, which means "bamboo mountain," because of all the bamboo that grows there. One of Fang-hsin's uncles runs a bamboo-stick factory on the first floor of her grandfather's house. The sticks are used to make things like bird cages and chopsticks. The young shoots of the bamboo are good to eat, and are used in many different dishes.

Sweet potatoes are grown here, too. Many people cook small chunks of sweet potato in their rice.

Fang-hsin's maternal grandparents (her mother's parents), whose family name is Lin, live outside Touliu, a village not far from Chushan.

The Lins are farmers and grow rice, bamboo shoots, vegetables, and fruits. They have both a mechanical plow and a water buffalo to plow the fields. More work can be done with a mechanical plow, so water buffalo are hardly ever used. But Grandfather Lin claims the ground of a field plowed by a water buffalo is smoother and more even.

Fang-hsin and her cousins take turns improving their skill at playing diabolo. Diabolo is an old Chinese toy that is popular among children in Taiwan. A hollow, dumbbell-shaped object, the diabolo, is set into a spin by wrapping a string that is tied to two sticks around the diabolo's middle, then pulling up and down on the sticks. Fang-hsin makes the diabolo go up and down the string, tosses it into the air and catches it while it is still spinning.

Fang-hsin has enjoyed visiting her grandparents and cousins, but summer vacation is coming to an end. Soon school will begin. Fang-hsin is excited about starting her first year of junior high school.

Made in Taiwan

You may have noticed a small sticker or tag on many of the things you buy, such as clothing, toys, electronic products, and umbrellas, that says "Made in Taiwan." Those items are part of Taiwan's international trade. International trade is the exchange of products or services between countries. Sending goods to other countries to be traded is called exporting.

Before the 1950s, Taiwan exported mainly agricultural products such as sugar and rice. In the 1950s, business-people in Taiwan started up factories to make products they hoped would be valuable in international trade. Taiwan's manufacturers started with things that were fairly easy to make and inexpensive to buy, such as plastic utensils and shoes. As Japan did years ago, Taiwan progressed from exporting knickknacks to clothes to professional sports equipment to electronic products and then to high-quality computers. Taiwan is changing the image of products that are "Made in Taiwan" from "cheap" to "high quality."

By exporting, Taiwan's manufacturers are able to sell far more goods than they could sell within their own country. Taiwan's thriving export trade has helped provide jobs and a higher standard of living for people in Taiwan.

Facts about Taiwan

Official Name: Republic of China

Capital: Taipei

Official language: Mandarin Chinese (other Chinese dialects such as Southern Fukienese and Hakka are common; a small aborigine population speaks Malay-related languages)

Form of Money: New Taiwan dollar (NT$)

Area: 13,970 square miles (36,180 square kilometers)
> The United States has about 255 times the area of Taiwan.

Population: 20,053,123 people
> The United States has about 12 times the population of Taiwan.

NORTH
AMERICA

SOUTH
AMERICA

EUROPE

ASIA

Taiwan

AFRICA

AUSTRALIA

Families the World Over

Some children in foreign countries live like you do. Others live very differently. In these books, you can meet children from all over the world. You'll learn about their games and schools, their families and friends, and what it's like to grow up in a faraway land.

Lerner Publications Company, 241 First Avenue North, Minneapolis, Minnesota 55401